"Knock, Knock", "Who's There"

"The Ultimate Joke and Knock, Knock Book"

James Reader

First published by James Reader 2023

Copyright © 2023 by James Reader

All rights reserved. No part of this publication may be reproduced, stored or transmitted in any form or by any means, electronic, mechanical, photocopying, recording, scanning, or otherwise without written permission from the publisher. It is illegal to copy this book, post it to a website, or distribute it by any other means without permission.

James Reader asserts the moral right to be identified as the author of this work.

James Reader has no responsibility for the persistence or accuracy of URLs for external or third-party Internet Websites referred to in this publication and does not guarantee that any content on such Websites is, or will remain, accurate or appropriate.

Designations used by companies to distinguish their products are often claimed as trademarks. All brand names and product names used in this book and on its cover are trade names, service marks, trademarks and registered trademarks of their respective owners. The publishers and the book are not associated with any product or vendor mentioned in this book. None of the companies referenced within the book have endorsed the book.

First edition

Contents

Introduction: 1

"Classic Knock, Knock Jokes" 2

   117 timeless Knock, Knock jokes for your amusement: 2

"Punny Wordplay" 29

   Awesome 1 liners 29

"Knock, Knock Jokes for All Ages" 38

   More and more and more......... 38

"Knock, Knock and Wordplay Jokes for Every Occasion" 47

   Halloween Knock, Knock Jokes 47

   Halloween Jokes 50

   Thanksgiving Knock, Knock Jokes 53

   Thanksgiving Jokes 56

   Christmas Knock, Knock Jokes 59

   Christmas Jokes 63

   Birthday Knock, Knock Jokes 66

   Birthday Jokes 70

"The Science of Laughter" 73

"Creating Your Own Knock, Knock Jokes" 74

   Choose a Theme or Subject: 74

   Set Up the Knock, Knock Format: 74

   Create a Playful Lead-In: 74

   Develop a Punchline: 75

- Practice and Refine: 75
- Keep It Short and Simple: 75
- Be Original: 75
- Consider Wordplay: 75
- Adapt to the Situation: 76
- Have Fun: 76
- Here's an example of a knock-knock joke with a Thanksgiving theme: 76

Conclusion: 77
Appendix: 78
Bonus: 78
- A bunch of Riddles to Exercise Your Brain! 78

Acknowledgments: 94

Introduction:

Prepare to embark on a delightful journey brimming with laughter, groans, and endless amusement as you open the door to "Knock, Knock, Who's There? A Giggle-Filled Joke Book." Within these pages lies a treasure trove of humor that is bound to have you in stitches with each and every page turn. This collection is a medley of classic knock-knock jokes, witty one-liners, and pun-tastic gems designed to tickle your funny bone.

Whether you're young or young at heart, this book is tailor-made for anyone who revels in a good chuckle. It offers a spectrum of humor, ranging from clever wordplay to delightful surprises, making it the ideal companion for any occasion. So, brace yourself to knock on the door of humor, and let the laughter cascade like a never-ending stream! Always remember, life is unequivocally brighter with a smile, and this book is your key to unlocking the door to boundless merriment.

Welcome to a world where laughter knows no boundaries, and where every knock at the door is an invitation to share a grin, a giggle, or a hearty guffaw. Are you ready to embark on this riotous journey filled with hilarity? Knock, knock...

Ultimately, this book's sole purpose is to summon smiles, laughter, and a sense of lightheartedness, rendering it the perfect addition to any bookshelf or a thoughtful gift guaranteed to brighten someone's day. Open the book and let the laughter flow freely! Highlight the universal allure of humor and its unique ability to bring sunshine into anyone'

"Classic Knock, Knock Jokes"

117 TIMELESS KNOCK, KNOCK JOKES FOR YOUR AMUSEMENT:

Knock, knock.

Who's there?
Cow says.
Cow says who?
No silly, a cow says "moo"!

Knock, knock.
Who's there?
Boo.
Boo who?
Don't cry; it's just a joke!

Knock, knock.
Who's there?
Lettuce.
Lettuce who?
Lettuce in; it's cold out here!

Knock, knock.
Who's there?
Justin.
Justin who?
Justin time for dinner!

Knock, knock.
Who's there?
Olive.
Olive who?
Olive you, and I miss you too!

Knock, knock.
Who's there?
Howard.
Howard who?
Howard you like to be wrapped as a gift?

Knock, knock.
Who's there?
Luke.
Luke who?
Luke through the peephole and find out!

Knock, knock.
Who's there?
Honeydew.
Honeydew who?
Honeydew you know how much I love you?

Knock, knock.
Who's there?
Ice cream.
Ice cream who?
Ice cream every time I see a scary movie!

Knock, knock.
Who's there?
Sam.
Sam who?
Same person who's been knocking on your door!

Knock, knock.
Who's there?
Alpaca.
Alpaca who?
Alpaca the suitcase; you load up the car!

Knock, knock.
Who's there?
Juan.
Juan who?
Juan a go swimming?

Knock, knock.
Who's there?
Hatch.
Hatch who?
Bless you!

Knock, knock.
Who's there?
Juan.
Juan who?
Juan to come in and hear a joke?

Knock, knock.
Who's there?
Ben.
Ben who?
Ben knocking for hours; open up!

Knock, knock.
Who's there?
Butter.
Butter who?
Butter open up or else!

Knock, knock.
Who's there?
Banana.
Banana who?
Knock, knock.
Who's there?
Banana.
Banana who?
Knock, knock.
Who's there?
Banana.
Banana who?
Knock, knock.
Who's there?
Orange.
Orange who?
Orange you glad I didn't say banana again?

Knock, knock.
Who's there?
Banana.
Banana who?
Banana split, so let me in!

Knock, knock.
Who's there?
Justin.
Justin who?
Justin time to see your smiling face!

Knock, knock.
Who's there?
Howard.
Howard who?
Howard you like to be my valentine?

Knock, knock.
Who's there?
Figs.
Figs who?
Figs the doorbell, it's not working!

Knock, knock.
Who's there?
Annie.
Annie who?
Annie thing you can do, I can do too!

Knock, knock.
Who's there?
Hal.
Hal who?
Hal will you know if you don't open the door?

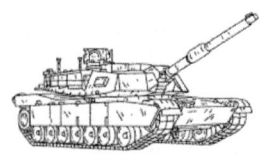

Knock, knock.
Who's there?
Tank.
Tank who?
You're welcome!

Knock, knock.
Who's there?
Alice.
Alice who?
Alice fair in love and war.

Knock, knock.
Who's there?
Says.
Says who?
Says me!

Knock, knock.
Who's there?
Honey bee.
Honey bee who?
Honey bee a dear and get that for me please!

Knock, knock.
Who's there?
A little old lady.
A little old lady who?
Hey, you can yodel!

Knock, knock.
Who's there?
Euripides.
Euripides who?
Euripides clothes, you pay for them!

Knock, knock.
Who's there?
Snow.
Snow who?
Snow use. The joke is over.

Knock, knock.
Who's there?
Hawaii.
Hawaii who?
I'm good. Hawaii you?

Knock, knock.
Who's there?
Leaf.
Leaf who?
Leaf me alone!

Knock, knock.
Who's there?
Woo.
Woo who?
Glad you're excited, too!

Knock, knock.
Who's there?
Who.
Who who?
I didn't know you were an owl!

Knock, knock.
Who's there?
wayer.
Anita who?
Let me in! Anita borrow something.

Knock, knock.
Who's there?
Water.
Water who?
Water you doing telling jokes right now? Don't you have things to do?

Knock, knock.
Who's there?
Annie.
Annie who?
Annie way you can let me in?

Knock, knock.
Who's there?
Nana.
Nana who?
Nana your business!

Knock, knock.
Who's there?
Needle.
Needle who?
Needle little help right now!

Knock, knock.
Who's there?
Taco.
Taco who?
Taco 'bout a funny joke!

Knock, knock.
Who's there?
Iran.
Iran who?
Iran here. I'm tired!

Knock, knock.
Who's there?
Amos.
Amos who?
A mosquito. Look, right there!

Knock, knock.
Who's there?
Some.
Some who?
Maybe some day you'll recognize me!

Knock, knock.
Who's there?
Cash.
Cash who?
Nah, I'm more into almonds.

Knock, knock.
Who's there?
Dozen.
Dozen who?
Dozen anyone want to let me in?

Knock, knock.
Who's there?
Dwayne.
Dwayne who?
Dwayne the sink. I need to use it!

Knock, knock.
Who's there?
Thermos.
Thermos who?
Thermos be a better way to get to you.

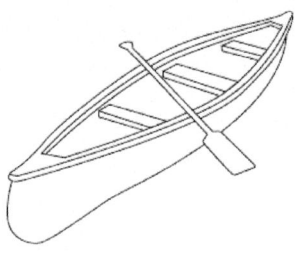

Knock, knock.
Who's there?
Canoe.
Canoe who?
Canoe come out now?

Knock, knock.
Who's there?
Razor.
Razor who?
Razor hands, this is a stick up!

Knock, knock.
Who's there?
Mustache.
Mustache who?
I mustache you a question.

Knock, knock.
Who's there?
Alec.
Alec who?
Alectricity. BUZZ!

Knock, knock.
Who's there?
Europe.
Europe who?
No I'm not!

Knock, knock.
Who's there?
Amarillo.
Amarillo who?
Amarillo nice person.

Knock, knock.
Who's there?
Orange.
Orange who?
Orange you glad you answered the door?

Knock, knock.
Who's there?
Harry.
Harry who?
Harry up and answer the door!

Knock, knock.
Who's there?
Owls.
Owls who?
Yes, they do!

Knock, knock.
Who's there?
Dozen.
Dozen who?
Dozen anyone want to let me in?

Knock, knock.
Who's there?
To.
To who?
Actually, it's to whom.

Knock, knock.
Who's there?
Candice.
Candice who?
Candice snack be eaten?

Knock, knock.
Who's there?
Police.
Police who?
Police let me in, it's chilly out!

Knock, knock.
Who's there?
Cher.
Cher who?
Cher would be nice if you opened the door!

Knock, knock.
Who's there?
Police.
Police who?
Police stop telling these silly jokes!

Knock, knock.
Who's there?
Stopwatch.
Stopwatch who?
Stopwatch you're doing and let me in!

Knock, knock.
Who's there?
Theodore.
Theodore who?
Theodore is stuck. Open up!

Knock, knock.
Who's there?
Spell.
Spell who?
W. H. O.

Knock, knock.
Who's there?
Robin.
Robin who?
Robin you. Give me your money!

Knock, knock.
Who's there?
Icy.
Icy who?
Icy you looking at me!

Knock, knock.
Who's there?
Voodoo.
Voodoo who?
Voodoo you think you are?

Knock, knock.
Who's there?
Alex.
Alex who?
Alex-plain later!

Knock, Knock
Who's there?
Nobel.
Nobel who?
Nobel…that's why I knocked!

Knock knock.
Who's there?
Abe Lincoln.
Abe Lincoln who?
You don't recognize me??!!

Knock knock.
Who's there?
Adorable.
Adorable who?
A-door-bell don't work, that's why I knocked!

Knock knock.
Who's there?
Goliath.
Goliath who?
Go lieth thee down, thou looks tired!

Knock knock.
Who's there?
Cargo
Cargo who?
CAR GO BEEP BEEP!

Knock knock.
Who's there?
Britney Spears.
Britney **Spears who?**
Knock knock.
Who's there?
Britney Spears. OOPS! I DID IT AGAIN!

Knock knock.
Who's there?
Daisy.
Daisy who?
DEY SEE ME ROLLIN THEY HATIN

Knock knock
Who's there?
Kenya.
Kenya who?
Kenya open the door?

Knock knock.
Who's there?
I eat mop.
I eat mop who?
Ew. That's gross

Knock, knock.
Who's there?
Cook.
Cook who?
Yeah, you do sound kinda crazy.

Knock knock.
Who's there?
A week.
A week who?
Yeah, we coo'.

Knock knock.
Who's there?
Wah.
Wah who?
It's-a me Mario!

Knock knock.
Who's there?
HIPAA.
HIPAA who?
I'm sorry, I'm not authorized to release that information.

Knock knock.
Who's there?
Control freak.
Con–
–Okay, now you say, "Control freak who?"

Knock knock.
Who's there?
Dejav.
Dejav who?
Knock, knock.
Knock knock.
Who's there?
Art.
Art who?
R2D2!

Knock knock.
Who's there?
Shamp.
Shamp who?
Does my hair really look that dirty?

Knock knock.
Who's there?
Doctor.
Doctor who?
Oh my gosh, I'm such a big fan!

Knock knock.
Who's there?
Hike.
Hike who?
I didn't know you liked Japanese poetry!

Knock knock.
Who's there?
Yah.
Yah who?
No, I use Google.

Knock knock.
Who's there?
Colin.
Colin who?
Colonization! Just kidding, colonizers don't knock before coming in.

Knock knock.
Who's there?
Opportunity, and I don't knock twice!

Knock knock.
Who's there?
Mikey.
Mikey who?
My key is lost — can you let me in?

Knock knock.
Who's there?
Cowsgo.
Cowsgo who?
No, cows go MOO!

Knock knock.
Who's there?
Pecan.
Pecan who?
Pecan somebody your own size!

Knock knock.
Who's there?
Fur.
Fur who?
Fur you, I can be anyone.

Knock knock.
Who's there?
Baby owl.
Baby owl who?
Baby, I'll see you later at my place.

Knock knock.
Who's there?
Disguise.
Disguise who?
Dis guy is your boyfriend? You could do so much better.

Knock knock.
Who's there?
Ida.
Ida who?
Surely, it's pronounced Ida-ho?

Knock knock.
Who's there?
Urine.
Urine who?
You're insecure; don't know what for.

Knock knock.
Who's there?
Bacon.
Bacon who?
Bae, can you give me a kiss?

Knock knock.
Who's there?
Wafer.
Wafer who?
Wafer me — I'm coming!

Knock knock.
Who's there?
Radio.
Radio who?
Radio not, here I come!

Knock knock.
Who's there?
Ariana Grande.
Ariana Grande who?
Okay, boomer!

Why did the chicken cross the road?
To get to the idiot's house.
Knock knock.
Who's there?
The chicken.

Knock knock.
Who's there?
Anna Partridge.
Anna Partridge who?
Anna Partridge in a pear tree!

Knock knock.
Who's there?
Madam.
Madam who?
Ma damn foot is stuck in the door!

Knock knock.
Who's there?
Omar.
Omar who?
Omargod, I have the wrong door!

Knock knock.
Who's there?
Leash.
Leash who?
Leash you could do is open the door!

Knock knock.
Who's there?
Breaking dawn.
Breaking dawn who?
I'm breaking dawn this door with my powerful vampire knocks!

Knock knock.
Who's there?
Beets.
Beets who?
Beets me!

Knock knock.
Who's there?
Interrupting pirate.
Interrupting pir–
ARRRRRRRRRRRR!

Knock knock.
Who's there?
Desiree.
Desiree who?
Desiree of sunshine shining through my window.

Knock knock.
Who's there?
Forget.
Forget who?
Forget you!

Knock knock.
Who's there?
A broken pencil.
A broken pencil who?
Nevermind, there's no point.

Knock knock.
Who's there?
Stopper.
Stopper who?
Stop'er! She's running off with your newspaper!

Knock knock.
Who's there?
Moron.
Moron who?
Moron that later, after these messages from our sponsors.

Knock knock.
Who's there?
Dewey?
Dewey who?
Dewey have to keep telling silly jokes?

Enjoy these classic knock-knock jokes, and share them with friends and family to brighten their day with a good laugh!

"Punny Wordplay"

AWESOME 1 LINERS

1. Why did the scarecrow win an award?
Because he was outstanding in his field.

2. What do you call a fish with no eyes?
Fsh.

3. What did one wall say to the other wall?
"I'll meet you at the corner."

4. Why don't scientists trust atoms?
Because they make up everything!

5. Why don't oysters donate to charity?
Because they are shellfish.

6. How does a penguin build its house?
Igloos it together!

7. Why don't seagulls fly over the bay?
Because then they'd be called "bagels"!

8. What did the bee use to brush its hair?
A honeycomb!

9. How do you catch a squirrel?
Climb a tree and act like a nut!

10. What do you call a bear in the rain?
A drizzly bear.

11. Why did the squirrel bring a ladder to the bar?
Because it heard the drinks were on the house.

12. What do you call a cow with no legs?
Ground beef.

13. What did the horse say after it tripped?
"Help! I've fallen, and I can't giddyup!"

14. Why did the chicken join a band?
Because it had the drumsticks!

15. Why do hummingbirds hum?
Because they don't know the words!

16. What did the snake say to the ladder?
"I can't charm you, but I can ladder you up!"

17. What do you call a dinosaur with an extensive vocabulary?
A thesaurus.

18. How do you make a hankie dance?
You put a little boogie in it!

19. Why did the dog sit in the shade?
Because he didn't want to be a hot dog!

20. What's a dog's favorite kind of pizza?
Pup-peroni!

21. How do you organize a fantastic space pr2d2y?
You "planet" to have a blast!

22. What kind of dog loves to take a bath?
A shampoo-dle!

23. Why did the frog take the bus to work?
His car got toad away.

24. What do you call a cat who can sing?
A soprano!

25. Why was the cat sitting on the computer?
Because it wanted to keep an eye on the mouse!

26. Why did the bicycle fall over?
Because it was two-tired.

27. Did you hear about the belt that got arrested?
It was holding up a pair of pants!

28. I'm friends with all electricians.
We have great current connections.

29. Did you hear about the kidnapping at the playground?
They woke up!

30. Why was the math book sad?
Because it had too many problems.

31. When the clock is hungry, it goes back four seconds.

32. Why did the tomato turn red?
Because it saw the salad dressing!

33. I'm reading a book on anti-gravity. It's impossible to put down.

34. What did the janitor say when he jumped out of the closet?
"Supplies!"

35. Did you hear about the guy who invented Lifesavers?
He made a mint!

36. What do you call a snowman in the summer?
A puddle.

37. I used to play piano by ear, but now I use my hands.

38. I'm friends with all the food in my fridge. I'm very cool.

39. I can't believe I got fired from the calendar factory. All I did was take a day off!

40. Did you hear about the cheese factory that exploded?
There was nothing left but de-brie!

41. I used to be a baker, but I couldn't make enough dough.

42. How do you organize a space party?
You "planet"!

43. I'm on a seafood diet. I see food, and I eat it.

44. What did the doctor say to the invisible man?
"I can't see you today."

45. Why do mathematicians make great detectives?
They follow the clues.

46. Did you hear about the red ship and the blue ship that collided?
Both crews were marooned.

47. Why did the scarecrow become a successful therapist?
Because he was outstanding in his field of psychology!

48. What kind of music do mummies listen to?
Wrap music.

49. Why did the scarecrow join a band?
Because it had the drumsticks!

50. What do you get when you drop a piano down a mine shaft?
A flat minor.

51. What do you call a snake that's 3.14 meters long?
A π-thon!97.

52. What do you call a bear with no teeth?
A gummy bear.

53. What's a skeleton's favorite room in the house?
The bathroom, of course!

54. Why did Adele cross the road?
To say hello from the other side.

55. What kind of concert only costs 45 cents?
A 50 Cent concert featuring Nickelback.

56. What did the grape say when it got crushed?
Nothing, it just let out a little wine.

57. I want to be cremated as it is my last hope for a smoking hot body.

58. Time flies like an arrow. Fruit flies like a banana

59. To the guy who invented zero, thanks for nothing.

60. I had a crazy dream last night! I was swimming in an ocean of orange soda. Turns out it was just a Fanta sea.

61. A crazy wife says to her husband that moose are falling from the sky. The husband says, it's reindeer.

62. Ladies, if he can't appreciate your fruit jokes, you need to let that mango.

63. Geology rocks but Geography is where it's at

64. What was Forrest Gump's email password?
1forrest1

65. Did you hear about the restaurant on the moon?
I heard the food was good but it had no atmosphere.

66. Can February March?
No, but April May.

67. Need an ark to save two of every animal?
I noah guy.

68. I don't trust stairs because they're always up to something.

69. Smaller babies may be delivered by stork but the heavier ones need a crane.

70. My grandpa has the heart of the lion and a lifetime ban from the zoo.

71. Why was Dumbo sad?
He felt irrelephant.

72. A man sued an airline company after it lost his luggage. Sadly, he lost his case.

73. I lost my mood ring and I don't know how to feel about it!

74. Yesterday, I accidentally swallowed some food coloring. The doctor says I'm okay, but I feel like I've dyed a little inside.

75. So what if I don't know what apocalypse means?
It's not the end of the world!

76. My friend drove his expensive car into a tree and found out how his Mercedes bends.

77. Becoming a vegetarian is one big missed steak.

78. I was wondering why the ball was getting bigger. Then it hit me.

79. Some aquatic mammals at the zoo escaped. It was otter chaos!

80. Never trust an atom, they make up everything!

81. Waking up this morning was an eye-opening experience.

82. Long fairy tales have a tendency to dragon.

83. What do you use to cut a Roman Emperor's hair?
Ceasers.

84. Knock, Knock
Who's there?
Sorry, wrong joke! There's a bunch more!

"Knock, Knock Jokes for All Ages"

MORE AND MORE AND MORE......

Knock, knock.
Who's there?
Iva.
Iva who?
I've a sore hand from knocking!

Knock, knock.
Who's there?
Ketchup.
Ketchup who?
Ketchup with me and I'll tell you!

Knock knock.
Who's there?
Needle.
Needle who?
Needle little money please.

Knock, knock.
Who's there?
Watson.
Watson who?
Watson TV right now?

Knock, knock.
Who's there?
Anee.
Anee who?
Anee one you like!

Knock, knock.
Who's there?
Dishes.
Dishes who?
Dish is a nice place!

Knock knock.
Who's there?
A herd.
A herd who?
A herd you were home, so here I am!

Knock, knock.
Who's there?
Avenue.
Avenue who?
Avenue knocked on this door before?

Knock, **knock.**
Who's there?
Althea.
Althea who?
Althea later alligator!

Knock, knock.
Who's there?
Arfur.
Arfur who?
Arfur got!

Knock knock.
Who's there?
Otto.
Otto who?
Otto know. I forgot.

Knock, knock.
Who's there?
Norma Lee.
Norma Lee who?
Norma Lee I don't knock on random doors, but I had to meet you!

Knock, knock.
Who's There?
Imma.
Imma who?
Imma getting older waiting for you to open up!

Knock, knock.
Who's there?
Yukon.
Yukon who?
Yukon say that again!

Knock, knock.
Who's there?
Viper.
Viper who?
Viper nose, it's running!

Knock, knock.
Who's there?
CD.
CD who?
CD person on your doorstep?

Knock, knock.
Who's there?
Claire.
Claire who?
Claire a path, I'm coming through!

Knock knock.
Who's there?
Roach.
Roach who?
Roach you a text. Did you get it?

Knock, knock.
Who's there?
Somebody too short to ring the doorbell!

Knock, knock.
Who's there?
Ivor.
Ivor who?
Ivor you let me in or I'll climb through the window.

Knock, knock.
Who's there?
Abbot.
Abbot who?
Abbot you don't know who this is!

Knock, knock.
Who's there?
Adore.
Adore who?
Adore is between us, so open it!

Knock, knock.
Who's there?
Noah.
Noah who?
Noah good place we can go hang out?

Knock, knock.
Who's there?
Kirtch.
Kirtch who?
God bless you!

Knock knock.
Who's There?
Impatient cow.
Impatient cow who?
Mooooo!

Knock, knock.
Who's there?
Sadie.
Sadie who?
Sadie magic word and I'll come in!

Knock, knock.
Who's there?
Iona.
Iona who?
Iona new toy!

Knock, knock.
Who's there?
Two knee.
Two knee who?
Two-knee fish!

Knock, knock.
Who's there?
Abby.
Abby who?
Abby birthday to you!

Knock, knock.
Who's there?
Cows go
Cows go who?
Cows don't go who, they go moo!

Knock, knock
Who's there?
Ben.
Ben who?
Ben knocking for 10 minutes!

Knock, knock.
Who's there?
Isabel.
Isabel who?
Isabel working?

Knock, knock.
Who's there?
Aida.
Aida who?
Aida sandwich for lunch today.

Knock, knock.
Who's there?
Scold.
Scold who?
Scold enough out here to go ice skating!

Knock, knock.
Who's there?
I am.
I am who?
Wait, you don't know who you are?

Knock, knock.
Who's there?
Amanda.
Amanda who?
A man da fix your door!

Knock, knock.
Who's there?
Al.
Al who?
Al give you a hug if you open this door!

Knock, knock.
Who's there?
Amish.
Amish who?
You're not a shoe!

Knock, knock.
Who's there?
Alfie.
Alfie who?
Alfie terrible if you don't let me in!

Knock, knock.
Who's there?
Alien.
Alien who?
Um, how many aliens do you know?

Knock, knock.
Who's there?
Andrew.
Andrew who?
Andrew a picture!

Knock, knock.
Who's there?
Dwayne.
Dwayne who?
Dwayne the tub, I'm dwowning.

Knock, knock.
Who's there?
Armageddon.
Armageddon who?
Armageddon a little bored. Let's go out.

"Knock, Knock and Wordplay Jokes for Every Occasion"

HALLOWEEN KNOCK, KNOCK JOKES

Knock, knock.
Who's there?
Ghost.
Ghost who?
Ghost away; you're scaring me!

Knock, knock.
Who's there?
Boo.
Boo who?
Don't cry; it's just Halloween fun!

Knock, knock.
Who's there?
Witch.
Witch who?
Witch one of you can lend me your broomstick?

Knock, knock.
Who's there?
Frank.
Frank who?
Frankenstein's monster! Don't be scared; I'm just looking for some spare parts!

Knock, knock.
Who's there?
Bat.
Bat who?
Batty to be out on Halloween night!

Knock, knock.
Who's there?
Dracula.
Dracula who?
Dracula bit me on the neck!

Knock, knock.
Who's there?
Mummy.
Mummy who?
Mummy told me to have a spook-tacular Halloween!

Knock, knock.
Who's there?
Pumpkin.
Pumpkin who?
Pumpkin up the Halloween decorations!

Knock, knock.
Who's there?
Spider.
Spider who?
Spider to wish you a creepy-crawly Halloween!

Knock, knock.
Who's there?
Zombie.
Zombie who?
Zombie glad it's Halloween!

I hope you have a "boo-tiful" Halloween filled with lots of laughter and treats!

HALLOWEEN JOKES

1. Why do ghosts go to the party?
Because they have no-body to dance with!

2. What do you call a mummy's favorite type of music?
Wrap music!

3. What kind of pants do ghosts wear?
Boo-jeans!

4. How do you mend a broken Jack-o'-lantern?
With a pumpkin patch!

5. What do you call a vampire with a cold?
A "sneeze-ula"!

6. How do you make a witch scratch?
Take away the "w"!

7. What did the skeleton order at the restaurant?
Spare ribs!

8. Why did the ghost go to the party?
Because he heard it was going to be a boo-last!

9. How do you make a skeleton laugh?
Tickle his funny bone!

10. What do you get when you cross a vampire with a snowman?
Frostbite!

11. What do you call a monster with no neck?
The lost neck monster!

12. What do you get when you drop a pumpkin?
Squash!

13. What's a vampire's least favorite room in the house?
The living room!

14. Why did the zombie go to school?
To improve his "dead"-ucation!

15. What's a skeleton's least favorite room in the house?
The living room!

16. What do you call a werewolf that barks instead of howling?
A "wherewolf"!

17. What did the black cat say on Halloween?
"Meow-oween!"

18. Why did the mummy take a vacation?
Because he was afraid he'd unwind!

19. Why didn't the skeleton cross the road?
Because he didn't have the guts!

20. What's a vampire's favorite fruit?
A blood orange!

21. Why did the monster apply for a job?
He wanted to make some "fiendish" money!

22. What do you call a ghost's true love?
His "ghoul-friend"!

23. Why did the scarecrow become a successful motivational speaker?
Because he was outstanding in his field!

24. How do you fix a broken pumpkin?
With a pumpkin patch!

I hope you enjoy these Halloween jokes, and may your Halloween be filled with spooky fun!

THANKSGIVING KNOCK, KNOCK JOKES

Knock, knock.
Who's there?
Butter.
Butter who?
Butter open up, it's Thanksgiving!

Knock, knock.
Who's there?
Mayflower.
Mayflower who?
Mayflower your heart be filled with gratitude this Thanksgiving!

Knock, knock.
Who's there?
Pumpkin.
Pumpkin who?
Pumpkin pie is the best part of Thanksgiving!

Knock, knock.
Who's there?
Olive.
Olive who?
Olive your Thanksgiving dishes are delicious!

Knock, knock.
Who's there?
Cranberry.
Cranberry who?
Cranberry sauce makes everything better on Thanksgiving!

Knock, knock.
Who's there?
Pilgrim.
Pilgrim who?
Pilgrim on eating a lot this Thanksgiving!

Knock, knock.
Who's there?
Gravy.
Gravy who?
Gravy you're here to celebrate Thanksgiving with us!

Knock, knock.
Who's there?
Stuffing.
Stuffing who?
Stuffing your face on Thanksgiving, just like me!

Knock, knock.
Who's there?
Corn.
Corn who?
Corn you believe it's Thanksgiving already?

Knock, knock.
Who's there?
Acorn.
Acorn who?
A-corn-y joke for Thanksgiving!

I hope these Thanksgiving knock-knock jokes add some laughter to your holiday festivities!

THANKSGIVING JOKES

1. "Why did the turkey join the band?
Because it had the drumsticks!"

2. "What do you call a turkey on the day after Thanksgiving?
Lucky!"

3. "I told my family I wanted to do something big for Thanksgiving, so we're having a sumo wrestler competition."

4. "Why was the math book sad on Thanksgiving?
Because it had too many problems."

5. "I'm thankful for elastic waistbands on Thanksgiving."

6. "If pilgrims were still alive today, what would they be famous for?
Their age!"

7. "What did the turkey say to the computer?
Google, Google, Google!"

8. "Thanksgiving is the only day you can enjoy stuffing without worrying about your figure."

9. "Why did the turkey sit next to the stuffing?
Because it wanted to be a part of the dressing!"

10. "What's a turkey's favorite dessert?
Peach gobbler!"

11. "Why did the cranberries turn red?
Because they saw the turkey dressing!"

12. "What kind of music did the pilgrims like?
Plymouth Rock!"

13. "Why did the turkey cross the road before Thanksgiving?
To get away from the people picking on it!"

14. "What do you get if you divide the circumference of a pumpkin by its diameter?
Pumpkin π!"

15. "I'm not a chef, but on Thanksgiving, I play one in the kitchen!"

16. "What did the mashed potatoes say to the sweet potatoes on Thanksgiving? '
You're such a yam-dandy!'"

17. "Why was the Thanksgiving soup so expensive?
It had 24 carrots!"

18. "What do you get when you drop a pumpkin?
Squash!"

19. "My family told me I'm terrible at telling Thanksgiving jokes, but I told them I'd give it a pie!"

20. "What did one pumpkin say to the other pumpkin?
'You're gourd-geous!'"

21. "Thanksgiving is the one day when you can count your blessings before they hatch!"

22. "I can't believe I'm already breaking out the 'fat pants' for Thanksgiving!"

23. "What do you get when you cross a turkey with a banjo?
A turkey that can pluck itself!"

24. "Why did the turkey apply for a job at the bakery?
Because it had the crust!"

I hope these Thanksgiving one-liners bring smiles to your holiday gatherings!

CHRISTMAS KNOCK, KNOCK JOKES

Knock, knock.
Who's there?
Snow.
Snow who?
Snow use knocking; come on in, it's chilly outside!

Knock, knock.
Who's there?
Jingle.
Jingle who?
Jingle all the way to a Merry Christmas!

Knock, knock.
Who's there?
Elf.
Elf who?
Elf us need a little Christmas right this very minute!

Knock, knock.
Who's there?
Ho, ho.
Ho, ho who?
Ho, ho-hope you have a wonderful Christmas!

Knock, knock.
Who's there?
Mary.
Mary who?
Mary Christmas to you and your family!

Knock, knock.
Who's there?
Wreath.
Wreath who?
Wreath yourself in holiday spirit!

Knock, knock.
Who's there?
Mistletoe.
Mistletoe who?
Mistletoe is where I want to be with you!

Knock, knock.
Who's there?
Candy.
Candy who?
Candy-cane be any sweeter than this Christmas!
Knock, knock.
Who's there?
Yule.
Yule who?
Yule-tide greetings to you and yours!

Knock, knock.
Who's there?
Santa.
Santa who?
Santa Claus is coming to town!

Knock, knock.
Who's there?
Ginger.
Ginger who?
Ginger-bread cookies for Santa, of course!

Knock, knock.
Who's there?
Sleigh.
Sleigh who?
Sleigh bells ring, are you listening?

Knock, knock.
Who's there?
Frosty.
Frosty who?
Frosty the Snowman, happy as can be!

Knock, knock.
Who's there?
Nutcracker.
Nutcracker who?
Nutcracker your way into the holiday spirit!

Knock, knock.
Who's there?
Rudolph.
Rudolph who?
Rudolph the Red-Nosed Reindeer, leading the way!

Knock, knock.
Who's there?
Mary.
Mary who?
Mary Christmas!

I hope these Christmas knock-knock jokes bring joy and laughter to your holiday celebrations!

CHRISTMAS JOKES

1. "Why was the math book sad during the holidays?
It had too many problems."

2. "What do you call a snowman with a six-pack?
An abdominal snowman!"

3. "What do you get if you cross a snowman and a dog?
Frostbite!"

4. "What's Santa's favorite pizza?
One that's deep-pan, crisp, and even."

5. "How do snowmen get around?
They ride an 'icicle'!"

6. "Why did the Christmas tree go to the barber?
It needed a trim."

7. "What do you call a snowman with a carrot nose and a banana smile?
Frosty the Snow-fruit!"

8. "Why was the ornament addicted to Christmas?
It had too many 'tree'-mendous memories."

9. "What did the gingerbread cookie use to fix his house?
Icing and gumdrops."

10. "What do you get when you cross a snowman and a vampire?
Frostbite!"

11. "What's Santa's favorite type of music?
Wrap music!"

12. "Why was the Christmas tree always in trouble?
It couldn't stop 'tree'-soning."

13. "How do you know when Santa's in the room?
You can sense his presents."

14. "What do you call an elf who sings?
A wrapper!"

15. "Why don't Christmas trees knit their own sweaters?
Because they're pines and needles!"

16. "Why did the gingerbread man go to the doctor?
He was feeling crumby."

17. "What do you get when you cross a snowman and a dog?
Frostbite!"

18. "What do you call a snowman in the summer?
A puddle!"

19. "Why was the snowman looking through the carrots?
He was picking his nose."

20. "What do you call a reindeer that tells jokes?
A 'comedian'!"

21. "Why was the computer cold during the winter?
It left its Windows open."

22. "What do you call a snowman with a sunburn?
A puddle!"

23. "Why do Christmas trees like knitting?
Because they're good at purling."

24. "What's an elf's favorite kind of music?
Wrap music!"

I hope these one-liners bring some festive laughter to your holiday season!

BIRTHDAY KNOCK, KNOCK JOKES

Knock, knock.
Who's there?
Alpaca.
Alpaca who?
Alpaca the balloons; it's your birthday!

Knock, knock.
Who's there?
Cow says.
Cow says who?
Cow says, "Happy birthday to you!"

Knock, knock.
Who's there?
Ice cream.
Ice cream who?
Ice cream every time I see your cake!

Knock, knock.
Who's there?
Olive.
Olive who?
Olive you, and I hope you have a wonderful birthday!

Knock, knock.
Who's there?
Lettuce.
Lettuce who?
Lettuce in; it's time to celebrate your birthday!

Knock, knock.
Who's there?
Woo.
Woo who?
Woo-hoo, it's your special day!

Knock, knock.
Who's there?
Cake.
Cake who?
Cake and ice cream are ready for your birthday party!

Knock, knock.
Who's there?
Candy.
Candy who?
Candy is sweet, but you're even sweeter on your birthday!

Knock, knock.
Who's there?
Present.
Present who?
Presenting you with a big birthday surprise!

Knock, knock.
Who's there?
Balloon.
Balloon who?
Balloon your way to a fantastic birthday!

Knock, knock.
Who's there?
Candles.
Candles who?
Candles are ready to be blown out; it's your birthday!

Knock, knock.
Who's there?
B-day.
B-day who?
B-day cake and party hats are waiting for you!

Knock, knock.
Who's there?
Wishes.
Wishes who?
Wishes for a very happy birthday to you!

Knock, knock.
Who's there?
Hooray.
Hooray who?
Hooray, it's your special day!

I hope these birthday knock-knock jokes add some fun to your celebration!

BIRTHDAY JOKES

1. "Age is merely the number of years the world has been enjoying you—happy birthday!"

2. "You know you're getting old when the candles cost more than the cake."

3. "Don't worry about your age; you're still the same fabulous person you've always been."

4. "They say that age is just a number, but in your case, it's a pretty big number!"

5. "You're not old; you're just retro!"

6. "Growing old is mandatory, but growing up is optional."

7. "At your age, 'getting lucky' means finding your car in the parking lot."

8. "Another year older, but definitely not wiser!"

9. "You're not over the hill; you're simply cresting the summit of life!"

10. "A birthday is just the first day of another 365-day journey around the sun. Enjoy the trip!"

11. "Why did the birthday cake visit the doctor? Because it was feeling a little crumby!"

12. "You're not getting older; you're increasing in value, like a fine wine."
13. "Age is a high price to pay for maturity."

14. "On your birthday, remember that you're not over the hill; you're on the hill—enjoy the view!"

15. "Getting older is like a classic book: the content is what matters, not the cover!"

16. "A birthday is the perfect time to stop and appreciate gravity."

17. "I'd bake you a cake, but I'm not sure how many candles I'd need!"

18. "Aging gracefully is like a work of art, and you are a masterpiece."

19. "You're not old; you're just retro!"

20. "You're not a year older; you're a year more fabulous!"

21. "May your birthday be filled with cake, laughter, and the people you love."

22. "You're like a fine wine; you get better with age."

23. "Birthdays are nature's way of telling us to eat more cake!"

24. "Age is a matter of feeling, not of years."

25. "Don't count the years; make the years count."

I hope these one-liners add some laughter to the birthday celebration!
Use all of these jokes to break the ice at parties or gatherings.

"The Science of Laughter"

Explore the psychological and physiological aspects of laughter.

Explain why humor is essential for mental and physical well-being.

Share real-life stories of laughter's healing power.

The Science of Laughter is a captivating journey into the intricate world of one of the most fundamental human expressions - laughter. This interdisciplinary field of study delves deep into the physiological, psychological, and social dimensions of laughter. Scientists investigate the release of endorphins and other neurochemicals accompanying laughter, uncovering its potent role as a natural mood enhancer. Furthermore, researchers analyze the social dynamics of laughter, exploring how it fosters connections among individuals, shapes language development, and enhances communication. By blending insights from psychology, neuroscience, and sociology, the Science of Laughter unravels the mysteries behind our laughter, its profound effects on us, and its pivotal role in shaping our human experience, providing a richer understanding of this universal and essential aspect of our lives.

"Creating Your Own Knock, Knock Jokes"

Creating your own knock-knock jokes can be a fun and creative process. Here are some steps to help you come up with your own knock-knock jokes:

CHOOSE A THEME OR SUBJECT:

Start by deciding on a theme or subject for your knock-knock joke. This could be related to a specific holiday, event, or topic that you find amusing.

SET UP THE KNOCK, KNOCK FORMAT:

The classic knock, knock joke format involves a simple dialogue structure:
You: "Knock, knock."
Recipient: "Who's there?"
You: "Punchline."

CREATE A PLAYFUL LEAD-IN:

The first part of your joke should be a playful or unexpected lead-in that sets the stage for the punchline. This is where you introduce the "who's there" element. Make sure it's related to your chosen theme or subject.

DEVELOP A PUNCHLINE:

The punchline is the funny or surprising part of your joke. It should be a word, phrase, or name that creates humor when paired with the lead-in. Be creative and use wordplay, puns, or unexpected associations.

PRACTICE AND REFINE:

Test your knock-knock joke on friends or family to see if it gets a good reaction. If it doesn't, you can refine the wording, timing, or punchline to make it funnier.

KEEP IT SHORT AND SIMPLE:

Knock-knock jokes work best when they are short and easy to understand. Avoid overly complex setups or punchlines.

BE ORIGINAL:

Try to come up with original jokes that are not commonly heard. Unique jokes tend to get better reactions.

CONSIDER WORDPLAY:

Wordplay is often at the heart of a good knock-knock joke. Think about how words sound, their multiple meanings, and how you can play with language for comedic effect.

ADAPT TO THE SITUATION:

You can create knock-knock jokes for specific occasions or tailor them to the people you're telling them to. For example, you can make jokes about a friend's interests or the current situation.

HAVE FUN:

The most important part of creating knock-knock jokes is to have fun with it. Don't take it too seriously, and enjoy the process of making people laugh.

HERE'S AN EXAMPLE OF A KNOCK-KNOCK JOKE WITH A THANKSGIVING THEME:

You: "Knock, knock."
Recipient: "Who's there?"
You: "Gravy."
Recipient: "Gravy who?"
You: "Gravy us another slice of pie, please!"

Remember that not every knock-knock joke will be a hit, and humor is subjective. Keep experimenting and trying different ideas until you find jokes that get the reaction you're looking for.

Conclusion:

Laughter possesses an extraordinary power to infuse joy and positivity into people's lives. It's a universal language that transcends boundaries and differences, connecting us through the shared experience of mirth. The sound of hearty laughter can lift spirits, mend wounds, and break down barriers. In the face of adversity or the challenges of everyday life, a good laugh can be a beacon of hope. It releases endorphins, relieves stress, and strengthens our emotional resilience. When we laugh together, we create bonds and lasting memories. The power of laughter reminds us that even in our darkest moments, there is lightness to be found, and it is often in the heartiest of laughs that we discover the strength to overcome life's obstacles and find the path to greater happiness.

Remember the most important thing of all is to share your favorite jokes with others and spread the gift of humor.

Appendix:

Bonus:

We forgot about riddles until we were done with the joke book. Hahaha. Here you go......

A BUNCH OF RIDDLES TO EXERCISE YOUR BRAIN!

1. I speak without a mouth and hear without ears. I have no body, but I come alive with the wind. What am I?
Answer: **An echo.**

2. I am taken from a mine and shut up in a wooden case, from which I am never released, and yet I am used by almost every person. What am I?
Answer: **Pencil lead/graphite.**

3. What comes once in a minute, twice in a moment, but never in a thousand years?
Answer: **The letter "M."**

4. The more you take, the more you leave behind. What am I?
Answer: **Footsteps**.

5. I am not alive, but I grow; I don't have lungs, but I need air; I don't have a mouth, but water kills me. What am I?
Answer: **Fire**.

6. I have keys but open no locks. I have space but no room. You can enter, but you can't go inside. What am I?
Answer: A keyboard.

7. I have cities but no houses, forests but no trees, and rivers but no water. What am I? **Answer**: A map.

8. I can fly without wings. I can cry without eyes. Wherever I go, darkness flees. What am I?
Answer: A cloud.

9. You see a boat filled with people. It has not sunk, but when you look again you don't see a single person on the boat. Why?
Answer: All the people were married.

10. I'm tall when I'm young and short when I'm old. What am I?
Answer: A candle.

11. What has keys but can't open locks?
Answer: A piano.

12. I can be cracked, made, told, and played. What am I?
Answer: A joke.

13. You see a boat filled with people. It has not sunk, but when you look again you don't see a single person on the boat. Why?
Answer: All the people were married.

14. I have a head, a tail, but never any legs. What am I?
Answer: A coin.

15. I have a heart that never beats, I can't run, but I have feet. What am I?
Answer: A refrigerator.

16. I have a head, a tail, but never any legs. What am I?
Answer: A coin.

17. The more you take, the more you leave behind. What am I?
Answer: Footsteps.

18. What has to be broken before you can use it?
Answer: An egg

19. I'm tall when I'm young, and I'm short when I'm old. What am I?
Answer: A candle

20. What month of the year has 28 days?
Answer: All of them

21. What is full of holes but still holds water?
Answer: A sponge

22. What question can you never answer yes to?
Answer: Are you asleep yet?

23. What is always in front of you but can't be seen?
Answer: The future

24. There's a one-story house in which everything is yellow. Yellow walls, yellow doors, yellow furniture. What color are the stairs?
Answer: There aren't any—it's a one-story house.

25. What can you break, even if you never pick it up or touch it?
Answer: A promise

26. What goes up but never comes down?
Answer: Your age

27. A man who was outside in the rain without an umbrella or hat didn't get a single hair on his head wet. Why?
Answer: He was towel.

28. What gets wet while drying?
Answer: A towel

29. What can you keep after giving to someone?
Answer: Your word

30. I shave every day, but my beard stays the same. What am I?
Answer: A barber

31. You walk into a room that contains a match, a kerosene lamp, a candle and a fireplace. What would you light first?
Answer: The match

32. A man dies of old age on his 25 birthday. How is this possible?
Answer: He was born on February 29.

33. I have branches, but no fruit, trunk or leaves. What am I?
Answer: A bank

34. What can't talk but will reply when spoken to?
Answer: An echo

35. The more of this there is, the less you see. What is it?
Answer: Darkness

36. David's parents have three sons: Snap, Crackle, and what's the name of the third son? **Answer**: David

37. I follow you all the time and copy your every move, but you can't touch me or catch me. What am I?
Answer: Your shadow

38. What has many keys but can't open a single lock?
Answer: A piano

39. What can you hold in your left hand but not in your right? **A**
Answer: Your right elbow

40. What is black when it's clean and white when it's dirty?
Answer: A chalkboard

41. What gets bigger when more is taken away?
Answer: A hole

42. I'm light as a feather, yet the strongest person can't hold me for five minutes. What am I?
 Answer: Your breath

43. I'm found in socks, scarves and mittens; and often in the paws of playful kittens. What am I?
Answer: Yarn

44. Where does today come before yesterday?
Answer: The dictionary

45. What invention lets you look right through a wall?
Answer: A window

46. If you've got me, you want to share me; if you share me, you haven't kept me. What am I?
 Answer: A secret

47. What can't be put in a saucepan?
Answer: It's lid

48. What goes up and down but doesn't move?
Answer: A staircase

49. If you're <u>running</u> in a race and you pass the person in second place, what place are you in?
 Answer: Second place

50. It belongs to you, but other people use it more than you do. What is it?
Answer: Your name

51. What has lots of eyes, but can't see?
Answer: A potato

52. What has one eye, but can't see?
Answer: A needle

53. What has many needles, but doesn't sew?
Answer: A Christmas tree

54. What has hands, but can't clap?
Answer: A clock

55. What has legs, but doesn't walk?
Answer: A table

56. What has one head, one foot and four legs?
Answer: A bed

57. 41. Riddle: What can you catch, but not throw?
Answer: A cold

58. 42. Riddle: What kind of band never plays music?
Answer: A rubber band

59. 43. Riddle: What has many teeth, but can't bite?
Answer: A comb

60. 44. Riddle: What is cut on a table, but is never eaten?
Answer: A deck of cards

61. 45. Riddle: What has words, but never speaks?
Answer: A book

62. What runs all around a backyard, yet never moves?
Answer: A fence

63. What can travel all around the world without leaving its corner?
Answer: A stamp

64. What has a thumb and four fingers, but is not a hand?
Answer: A glove

65. What has a head and a tail but no body?
Answer: A coin

66. Where does one wall meet the other wall?
Answer: On the corner

67. What building has the most stories?
Answer: The library

68. What tastes better than it smells?
Answer: Your tongue

69. What has 13 hearts, but no other organs?
Answer: A deck of cards

70. It stalks the countryside with ears that can't hear. What is it?
Answer: Corn

71. What kind of coat is best put on wet?
Answer: A coat of paint

72. What has a bottom at the top?
Answer: Your legs

73. What has four wheels and flies?
Answer: A garbage truck

74. I am an odd number. Take away a letter and I become even. What number am I?
Answer: Seven

75. If two's company, and three's a crowd, what are four and five?
Answer: Nine

76. What three numbers, none of which is zero, give the same result whether they're added or multiplied?
Answer: One, two and three

77. Mary has four daughters, and each of her daughters has a brother. How many children does Mary have?
Answer: Five—each daughter has the same brother.

78. Which is heavier: a ton of bricks or a ton of feathers?
Answer: Neither—they both weigh a ton.

79. Three doctors said that Bill was their brother. Bill says he has no brothers. How many brothers does Bill actually have?
Answer: None. He has three sisters.

80. Two fathers and two sons are in a car, yet there are only three people in the car. How?
Answer: They are a grandfather, father and son.

81. The day before yesterday I was 21, and next year I will be 24. When is my birthday?
Answer: December 31; today is January 1.

82. A little girl goes to the store and buys one dozen eggs. As she is going home, all but three break. How many eggs are left unbroken?
Answer: Three

83. A man describes his daughters, saying, "They are all blonde, but two; all brunette but two; and all redheaded but two." How many daughters does he have?
Answer: Three: A blonde, a brunette and a redhead

84. If there are three apples and you take away two, how many apples do you have?
Answer: You have two apples.

85. A girl has as many brothers as sisters, but each brother has only half as many brothers as sisters. How many brothers and sisters are there in the family?
Answer: Four sisters and three brothers

86. What five-letter word becomes shorter when you add two letters to it?
Answer: Short

87. What begins with an "e" and only contains one letter?
Answer: An envelope

88. A word I know, six letters it contains, remove one letter and 12 remains. What is it?
Answer: Dozens

89. What would you find in the middle of Toronto?
Answer: The letter "o"

90. You see me once in June, twice in November and not at all in May. What am I?
Answer: The letter "e"

91. Two in a corner, one in a room, zero in a house, but one in a shelter. What is it?
Answer: The letter "r"

92. I am the beginning of everything, the end of everywhere. I'm the beginning of eternity, the end of time and space. What am I?
Answer: Also the letter "e"

93. What 4-letter word can be written forward, backward or upside down, and can still be read from left to right?
Answer: NOON

94. Forward I am heavy, but backward I am not. What am I?
Answer: The word "not"

95. What is 3/7 chicken, 2/3 cat and 2/4 goat?
Answer: Chicago

96. I am a word of letters three; add two and fewer there will be. What word am I?
Answer: Few

97. What word of five letters has one left when two are removed?
Answer: Stone

98. What is the end of everything?
Answer: The letter "g"

99. What word is pronounced the same if you take away four of its five letters?
Answer: Queue

100. I am a word that begins with the letter "i." If you add the letter "a" to me, I become a new word with a different meaning, but that sounds exactly the same. What word am I?
Answer: Isle (add "a" to make "aisle")

101. What word in the English language does the following: The first two letters signify a male, the first three letters signify a female, the first four letters signify a great, while the entire world signifies a great woman. What is the word?
Answer: Heroine

102. What is so fragile that saying its name breaks it?
Answer: Silence.

103. What can run but never walks, has a mouth but never talks, has a head but never weeps, has a bed but never sleeps?
Answer: A river

104. Speaking of rivers, a man calls his dog from the opposite side of the river. The dog crosses the river without getting wet, and without using a bridge or boat. How?
Answer: The river was frozen.

105. What can fill a room but takes up no space?
Answer: Light

106. If you drop me I'm sure to crack, but give me a smile and I'll always smile back. What am I?
Answer: A mirror

107. The more you take, the more you leave behind. What are they?
Answer: Footsteps

108. I turn once, what is out will not get in. I turn again, what is in will not get out. What am I?
Answer: A key

109. People make me, save me, change me, raise me. What am I?
Answer: Money

110. What breaks yet never falls, and what falls yet never breaks?
Answer: Day, and night

111. What goes through cities and fields, but never moves?
Answer: A road

112. I am always hungry and will die if not fed, but whatever I touch will soon turn red. What am I?
Answer: Fire

113. The person who makes it has no need of it; the person who buys it has no use for it. The person who uses it can neither see nor feel it. What is it?
Answer: A coffin

114. A man looks at a painting in a museum and says, "Brothers and sisters I have none, but that man's father is my father's son." Who is in the painting?
Answer: The man's son

115. With pointed fangs I sit and wait; with piercing force I crunch out fate; grabbing victims, proclaiming might; physically joining with a single bite. What am I?
Answer: A stapler

116. I have lakes with no water, mountains with no stone and cities with no buildings. What am I?
Answer: A map

117. What does man love more than life, hate more than death or mortal strife; that which contented men desire; the poor have, the rich require; the miser spends, the spendthrift saves, and all men carry to their graves?
Answer: Nothing

Keep your eye out for our next Joke Book. It will be hard to match, but we will do it!!!!!!!!

Acknowledgments:

Thank you to all friends and family who helped listen to all of the jokes in this book. It probably was hard, but someone has to do it.

And last but not least, thank you for buying our joke book. Without you it wouldn't be possible!

Printed in Great Britain
by Amazon